My Little
Book of Romance

MICHAEL HART

This document is published by Lee's Press and Publishing Company located in the United States of America. It is protected by the United States Copyright Act, all applicable state laws and international copyright laws. The information in this document is accurate to the best of the ability of Michael Hart at the time of writing. The content of this document is subject to change without notice.

ISBN-13: 9798332607585
Paperback

TODAY

Talk to femmes so many... to be found. With a hope-that is mine... To be with a one for who-to hold–my heart only can go-to a touch of hers next to mine. I feel so alone many times...have and will only give a love so deep in my feel... To look to her eyes she takes a steal...My life and hers would be so real...There I am a man who I be...Into a look to her, here I feel...The fire is what I need...to be complete... and want to show her a life ...Never regret...She is there in my heart...I walk to her...Seeing the bright of 'morrows quest and make me be a man not alone but, in her hold... These things that I ask with most respect... I give her my heart-my soul of love... Will always be... So, hold me now and never go...I love you right- my woman dear...you will know.

MIKOL

TODAY

Look to the sky so Velvet To find me...I am there. To hold your good and bad. To hear you when you are alone Cold. A night to know me and all I possess. The words come free to help you in need. The words you see...Come from so deep inside of me. For all to see when I can show. My Love of Love is what they be. I feel so much never the bad is why I want to be so Emotionally. Shall I want a few years more. I can only hope that Love...Will all ways be here. And can con- quer you see the evil that man can bring to a world. I know not of this evil, for I Love...and will always be- a' giving to all who need. My source is from a place...They call the Power of Light. I have been sent here to show you what Love is... A name you Balk until you know...Tis' Me the real Michael.

MIKOL

TODAY 2

We walk to a place not far from here. a walk not meant to speak. For, in our eyes the passion we seek. our souls to know - the love runs deep. I feel a need to hold on. for, I fear none of the unknown. To see the love embodied to me. A blessing to give to all who need. A door for them is always open... A love I will give and never be broken.

MIKOL

TODAY 3

From a love so deep with want I need.
to travel slow-my seek is to know...
I can love and show a love so dear...
I want to keep. My heart says go.
I want to know...can I go?
Or, should I think before my heart?
Save my heart from a tatter?
Cannot let it be battered...
Cannot let it go to anywhere....
the way of most. For I be a man who sees...
a woman with honesty.
Eyes are bright a light so rare...beauty she is to my
heart-safe in her love...
I be in her love romantically...
Sharing a warmth many wish to feel...
it is me and her, a quest we are on...
To show them love and all ways be real.

MIKOL

TODAY 4

A song o' the night-nearer to light and bright to the touch of our souls — aglow - see through the words... if we shall meet? Leave 'nary a goodbye, only good-night. True to our plight missing romance-of lacking we share-for it is right-we tarry a meet and wonder if we dare? Go to a place we call romantically.

MIKOL

TODAY 5
OH MY, OH MY

*My hopes and wants
to dream of one...
adorned...she walks from
my dreams to be with me
I see her on my arm-we go-
they look...see us...and all of our charm.
They feel-they see- we are of one-out-
and know a bond we are... No one will dare.
A share of the night-kisses by light and
happy we are-not of any worry...
our time is long we hold each.
continue our touch to our hearts...
only we know...though we must go...
rest we will...the time
fleets and I take her there.
To stay we try...to hold each in our look....
a kiss so shy.... but never a goodbye.*

MIKOL

TODAY 6
O SWEET

The days I spend with you will always be so close to my thoughts. My soul. My heart. I know I move too fast. I would hope with your touch, you could help me to slow. And we could always be...only as one. The ways... it should be. My Love for no one but you. My heart for all of You... Only, you need to take it and feel its Power. The Love, Yes, Only Love it has for you. So much I can give you without fear. I know who I am. Who I can be. And, where I am going. I need a friend to share This Life's Love...To see the sun set to a darkness...With a fire to light the darkness in our passionate eyes. To see a life full of goodness. A life full of Laughing. To only be you the special one in my heart. If I have done all of these...Then this is a place to start...To find us as one.... Just hold me.

MIKOL

TODAY 7
TITLES

The moon boils the tide...light bright to our sight. ...As the waves MAKE SWEET LOVE TO THE SAND WE WALK THERE... HAND IN HAND...AN EMBRACE WE TAKE. A KISS TO THE SEA- LOVERS WE ARE...AS THE SAND AND SEA. A BOND WE SHARE, AS WARM AS A 1000 SUNS...WE GO ON TO A PLACE WE KNOW...HOLDING ON...A ROCK TO GAZE OUT TO ETERNITY AND THEN OUR EYES MEET AS THE SAND AND SEA...

MIKOL

TODAY 8

If I can paint ...you could hear the colours. And to be a musician you can see the music. Since I write words... you can feel the passion of the words soaring through your soul.... so deep you know close to you... they flow as a spring to the surface for us to drink with our eyes... we think. You feel the words... and you know... of love not many can feel so I show these words to all only from my being... to help love lost know it is not far to go...look to their soul to find light of colours you hear.

MIKOL

TODAY 9
SO NICE

Our hands locked as our hearts dream on... Our space is us never to release... for a bond we are... so right, so true... this is the love we share... to walk with you and look... to your warmth... A smile brightens the most gloomy of thoughts... eyes so bright to look into them with so much glee... to hold you now as our love grows strong... we are one and no one can see... for ours is ours and always be... a walk we take our hands locked... as we embrace the coming of shimmer for the sun sets... to our day is through we kiss and hold a love so true... now we dream of our embrace... my head held close to your breast... I never want to leave... for the safest I be... we can see this real love, and no one can take... we are one and locked as our hands in such a gentle embrace.

MIKOL

Whisper the Walk our voices impart... A glow of thoughts our souls embark... Our words flow and we simmer to delights of times we want and bask in the light... Looking to the moon on a summers' night... Feelings of safe we talk of the ways... For us to take... Our journey of thought... Never stops. Our love of the closeness is warmth to our silent muse... As if we are only the two who are here... For nothing we can lose... See and our tune to each of Loves' song... We can only speak... We are really one... As we only can be Lovers Yes, we are, as they see... Wishing they must be in our steps of our whispering walks we take nightly... Lovers so close our souls to keep... Our secrets only for us to feast... They can see, Yes, we love of Great love and know for us... Our whisper of walk the light we shine of Love 'tween no one can see... So, close our Whisper the Walk.

MIKOL

TODAY 11
A Huh "Sho" Nuff

...Of many things lost and gained...Held some femmes to a greater dawn – They moved on- Can Not say why... For in their mind the truth—lies... Greener Parcels? And Finer times? Tis' once in a day... A woman passed my path... Woman not of need But, so seem the same wants as mine. Made the call... She showed me her siren... Was so hearing her and could not remember my number o' reach. Looking, we be of eachs' wants... For, of the Need-we are about not.

MIKOL

TODAY 12
AND YOU WOULD MELT

...Love so few... behold in my life...
Never known...
She walks I see near'er my sight...
My hand in her's and all is right.
Warmth to the feel... And oh, so bright!
We walk to our place to steal this night...
A holdn' though we kiss our lips...
Feel the wet the fire is ignited...
Two souls unite such blissful delight...
One we be our embrace to see...
Tis' of Loves around us...
Feel our free...
Lovers' who know.
just lust has no foundry...
In this we are of Loves' bound...

MIKOL

TODAY 13
MY WISH

Of these days I walk alone. Feel the ways me' heart wants to go. Not a tear I weep 'less I'm about to sleep. So many who see... I of magical naught... Heavy thoughts so outweigh my spirit of who I am... Where I be going... How will I get there? No answer. My mind soars so many places... Just a hand to hold when it is cold... Her feet of chill at my back to the warmest of them gets. A walk in the brisk... She is not by me... I wish. A laughter I keep to my own. Wishing for the day to share all of Loves' wondrous ways... To hold her voice to mine' ears...To hope her thoughts...To see her smile...Hear her sigh of flowers abundant in--her hands... To be her wishes come about. Of times of good and bad we are forging as one... To touch her hair in a way for her to feel love... Not of need, for her of give to me and so mine tonight... If she were only by my side... So, I, walk alone another day... My sights are true... As my thoughts of a wish... If she were here? Of thee this I wish not so much to ask for. Know not I. For of true I am only. And just a chance... She is looking for me... I am here where you thought... You could not find me.

MIKOL

TODAY 14
MY WISH

A want of loves' gems we seek... A hand to hold... A kiss with only a one' to embrace. I look to find her side by mine... Our eyes ever looking forward as we walk and never wonder-backward. Too many sights of our gaze... Our hearts filled to flowing with romance... So long we have looked for loves in them.... Was never the right... Tho' we searched for true-day and night...now, so blue... how could I find you? Amongst all that we seek of a hold we keep... So deep a kiss, a touch and a look we be... to always go on our seek... Places that must eventually bring us to happy... For we have looked so far so vast as the sand and sea... Now we walk together our hands finally in the clasp... Kick about the stories in the sand of ships lost through the days... Their parts remain laid at our feet... We were as the ships of many a yore... Lost at sea - As we searched for each among the ones... Still, we walk along that shore... and kiss to a longing for we have found "we" ... Although lost til' our eyes met and we felt the electricity... and, of chemical bond finally we are one and look out beyond...

MIKOL

TODAY 15
AWWW.... TIS LOVE

For, to give her the flowers of mine heart... Spending an hour with her peace... To look-Her eyes at me... Dreams of holds so far and between. Times we are in Romance at our feet... With walks together our arms held most... None have shown more than she... Is this a dream? Or we do feel the love we seek? Feel the strong they see our embrace we takes'... Kisses sweet of nectars wishes and grace... So many to try a love of found... Only to go sideways bound... We try to build our new... Can they see? It's you and me on a way to loves' many paths... Our hopes of longing to be as one... We start this new in lovers' romance to chase and see of the many chemistries... We look and amazed our dawn has begun... Of wants taken... The night we are within shimmers delight—Our hearts unite... Closeness to feel... Warmth's we steal... To the each they see of hearts mingled... Wish they do... A moment we are gone now. They witnessed Love. So, in their hearts: Feels of Joy... They know we are of Love and never the coy...

MIKOL

TODAY 16
GET A KLEENEX

……Moments her touch to Mine Watch as close the hair she twines…Her face she puts…A glance for me…I shy to away…Gazing Looks to more…Again she sees me – For must I be in the glass…She trusts to make her beauty…Lie to think – She is doing this for me? Her caring wince…A nod of glow…She is most to the happy…Her walk away leaves me ponder…What I'd Love to wander through her trusses and never be found beyond yonder?

MIKOL

TODAY 17
EFFECT A POEM

Let me discover what delights you.
Allow me the pleasure of passions' search.
With whispered breath and a gentle brush.
Savor the freedom, the moment...the rush.

Trust me to clear the mortar and stone.
To explore the music of your soul.
Celebrate a joy, a hope ...a start.
Open to me your reclusive heart.

Banish the pangs of your hungers' past.
Dark shadows of hurt and dismay.
Welcome a friend, a lover, a guide.
And begin a spectacular ride.

Now close your eyes and empower me.
To share the anticipation and the need.
Exalt, regale in a sensuous bliss.
The taste, the sound, the feel... the kiss.

Relish today's spontaneous feast.
With laughter and glorious detail.
As the patience of time waits anew.
Offer to me the wonder of you.
Lay down with me and embrace the warmth.
A moment seized as hearts collide.
A clash of cymbals. A stroke of heat.
A flourish of melody, of harmony... of sweet.

TODAY 18
WEDNESDAY

If I can paint... you could hear the colours... for, I, to be a musician you could see the music ... I write words from the soul- so deep to know. Hold them close to you -and they flow as a spring to the surface for us to   drink with our eyes... we think.   Feel the words and you know - of the love I desire...– the words only show.

MIKOL

TODAY 19
LOVE

Her thoughts of keep... Loves' so sweet... Nights a' many—Hearts beat---Sounds serene—Simple holds.... flesh warm - Melted as one... Our lives as the surprise delight... Feelings unite... So, close our tight. Eyes locked... As do our souls... Never relent to any space.... can ever, never come between... Lovers' great so felt to us.... Wish to linger and never know apart to be.... For, in your arms I only want to know... Lips caress with kisses might---Want to only go—Where you're touch finds me---So Right.

MIKOL

TODAY 20
YES!

The midst of a mist
Soft touches... Her eyes grace to my core
Of being in her hold
Her Love so much to me
As gold --- Mine' heart knows...
Oh, beauty her sweet touch warms me
In so inside I feel she makes my life whole
I wander to wonder will she come
As close to just caress me.
Thoughts o' mine so beckon ---
To wish this of greatest hope....

MIKOL

TODAY 21
GOSH OH ME, OH MY

Shimmering dance o' lights of night
Wonder the thought as I walk near you—
Then our kisses do gentle So meaning of be they
A chance our meet we took to see
Discover each's' greatest delights
Went the ways to Lovers' our place
Felt the surge my head to your breast
Holding the warmth, you bring to my soul
In your touch sincere and most bold
Ways this heart will never hath known
Until you – who has never seen
I to you give my all...Want so little
When I gaze a sight to you my heart feels the safe –
As your arms circle me when we embrace to a
Night of lights Loving you

MIKOL

TODAY 22
YOU AND ME

Though away distance of sight...
Thoughts my mind
only soar with
roaring moments...
Mine' heart all
ways to yours---Time
O' good we be to our own...
In lovers' dance we embrace... A
Warmth---Only ours of share...
To kiss we do and,
The all want to stare... Of many times
Our dare to chance--- At loves' many ways...
choices and prance... To only pray
Our fates of good... We see in each so much the of we
could---
We would. A life we share our hold we are---Never
part
For ONE we are... In our sight the light we always
be...
Oh, Baby, it's just you and me.

MIKOL

TODAY 23
TO FIND YOU

*Dawn our days fallen in
Loves' warmth---Touches our hearts of
Feelings this way... Inside
Of deep more emotions play...
Our close we know---Not many
Can say... Smiles my heart feelings
Of you... Sent to me my ways...
Our eyes touch never known of
Blue... In an endless trance---
In an embrace we take to feel
This Love---Above all whispered words
we dearest Lover's chant... To
Soothe a longing---Our evermore...
Oh, Lovely romance---Baby all to yours...
And, you to read---Of hope to show
My Love is true and so pure...
All I ever want to do Oh baby of sweet---
Is hold you in my arms as I do in my heart...*

MIKOL

TODAY 24
GLOVES

As the night gloves the day...
Of moonlight walks we bay...
Of kisses we take in so
many ways...
Hair of yours glances
my being Giving me all my wants
and so many desires...needs
My deep thoughts
of you I ponder...
Oh, my heart sings softly...
When not with you---
Near your side...I dream
of the hours we are...
Near'r side by mine...
Our many nights---Our
words brush each...
Oh, Baby---Please in your hold---
I only want to be.

TODAY 25
SOFT TOUCHES

*Embrace our days with love filled ways...
Holds complete---So you feel our passions... Unite as
one for who we are... These times we need---In truest
love deeds... Of words we touch with lips our must...
To hear them---Say them---we do so with greatest
trust... Oh, woman I am in most respect...Please see
me an honest being...With words not of neglect....
Lucky I am and know this of true... The truth your
heart finds me... Please hold me close and never go...
Mine heart only knows... Mine head near your
breast...*

MIKOL

TODAY 26
EMOTIONS

Look to the sky on a clear cool night...
See the diamonds there
Resting in velvet... Reach up and
Take one... Hold the diamond close to
Your soul... For the diamond is a gift of a
Thousand suns... Walk on with me more...
To gaze or' the blue... We go to a place we know...
Watching the sea make
Sweetest love to the sand...
As we look out to all of our
Eternal bliss... Hearts o' ours in beats of zeal...
We all ways hope this is real... Our hearts filled
With loves' most emotions... Our love is now...
The close we are showing...

MIKOL

TODAY 27
MIST OF BLISS

Romance is the melting two into one...
For thee fire to burn---
A spark must ignite... Two
Hearts touch to equal one...
Passionate wants to each they seek...
Needs come and go... Many
Nights of kissed enamored... Eyes
See so the feel... A mist of visions---
Many quests... Blur the malice so many of
Them reel... In the heart---Look to feel Loves'
Greatest powers... Unlock them for, you must
There you will see the feel you need...
The powers of Love are yours---You
Only need to look... They are there only
If you want them... Just feel them to your
Soul.

MIKOL

TODAY 28
SWEETER NECTARS

Of dreaming slumbers...
You walk to my heart... Seeing me wanting
Your touch... And beg for your taste...
Lips yours of honey... Sweeter nectars
I have not known... Passion's flow and twist
From every want... Unbridled
Emotions now are heard... In
Our one---Love rings real...
Holding you as I only know.... How
My arms feel... Your warmth
On such this cold, cool night
Must awaken... For, now you nearest
My side... To kiss your body and soul---
And your lips are of great wanton.

MIKOL

TODAY 29
THOU IT SHINES

Touches to me... Your eyes in
Mine... Of hearts and one our being
So true... Romance we are truest
To form... See how it shines...
Met we did and never looked back...
Our sights we see in music and words...
Precise to gather our thoughts in a
Clamor... We listen to feel our ways of them
Banter... In an embrace we take of serious
Holding you now my soul of the
Happy... For you have made me a man
Of being... When once was lost and
Now you have found me...

MIKOL

TODAY 30
SUNDAY

The moon boils the tide...light bright to our sight.
...As the waves make sweet love to the sand...
we walk there...hand in hand...an embrace we take.
a kiss to the sea- lovers we are...as the sand and sea.
a bond we share, as warm as 1000 suns...we go on
to a place we know...holding on...a rock to gaze out
to an eternity and then our eyes meet as the sand
and sea...

MIKOL

MONDAY

If I can paint ...you could hear the colours.
And for to be a musician you can see the music.
Since I write words...you can feel the passion
Of the words soaring through your soul....
So deep you know.
close to you...they flow
as a spring to the surface for us to
drink with our eyes... we think.
You feel the words...and you know... of love
not many can feel so I show these words
to all only from my being...
to help love lost know it is not far to go...
look to their soul to find light of colors you hear.

MIKOL

TODAY 31
OUR FIRES

In our hearts the feelings make
Our souls unite to a touch only we our
the promise we make eyes show all
emotions guide the tact we take
the love we keep and never
fades the feel to want
our needs are asked...
of who and hope the time never pass...
being with you is my only desire
to hold your warmth with such admire
a kiss of lips heated by our fires
the one we have so sweet to see I only
want you will you marry me? Small the words that
mean
a life to share and love so abundantly my heart
skips when you walk to
me a hold I want to eternity...
can you see the love shining from me? A light so
bright
it's you that does this to me
oh, this love I want to give you and more
can't you see its me to you for one? The
truth is here take from me and never
want another for all I am who can
deliver to smell your sweet of fragrance
when you're near'r my heart
blossoms to know your devotion of kind---it's there.

MIKOL

TODAY 32
A WOMAN

The words shared are warm
The touches felt are a fire
That burns deep inside
How can this be?
To not have placed my eyes
To yours until now and a day
To feel what there
is... this fire that burns
To hold you and know
it's real and true
A touch of emotions
that passions emote
How can I hold you without
Knowing the feel of
your soul til' I heard
The words soft, from you, woman
You, have given to me?
Please no changes of you
That you might want
For, tis' you I am
beginning to know
And only want more of this.
Oh, Woman of Sweet...

MIKOL

TODAY 33
WE MEET

*Oh, tantric bliss as we
are finally found Our hearts unite too the
sound of one. Our search has been with dents
to our souls Then we see a light that begins
our story of intimate goals Touching you as
the love is made knowing well this is real
and being true our sought Our love may shine
it's brightest when our kisses are felt
Passions are must to hold you're
soul Mine eyes see you in plentiful harvest
of a longing we can finally end
The moment you said "Hello", There
was a dawn to me you're smiles enveloped?
thoughts and emotions Could I have
found the one I seek? You were there
searching as me. To be awakened now
in loves' glory Oh how I have wanted
this so deep and giving. To hold you only one
the night is stormy. These days of have
want and need. Now you are there in
my arms indeed. Holding you entwined
with lovers, forever's' want. Kiss me
twice so we know
our love is here and only our place
shared for us to go.*

MIKOL

9 7 9 8 3 3 5 4 1 5 7 6 7